SAVING
ENDANGERED SPECIES

by Todd Kortemeier

12 STORY LIBRARY

www.12StoryLibrary.com

12-Story Library is an imprint of Peterson Publishing Company and Press Room Editions.

Produced for 12-Story Library by Red Line Editorial

Photographs ©: Cathy Withers-Clarke/Shutterstock Images, cover, 1; Robson Abbott/ Shutterstock Images, 4; FloridaStock/Shutterstock Images, 5; Heather Lucia Snow/ Shutterstock Images, 7; US Fish and Wildlife Service, 8, 17, 23; Steven Cole/Shutterstock Images, 9; Nopparat Nakhamhom/Shutterstock Images, 10; brentawp/iStockphoto, 11; Maggy Meyer/Shutterstock Images, 13; Hung Chung Chih/Shutterstock Images, 15, 29; Heiko Kiera/Shutterstock Images, 16, 28; think4photop/Shutterstock Images, 18; Richard Whitcombe/Shutterstock Images, 19; BLM Nevada, 20; Manny Crisostomo/Sacramento Bee/ZUMAPRESS.com, 21; Scott E. Nelson/Shutterstock Images, 22; Signature Message/ Shutterstock Images, 25; vitstudio/Shutterstock Images, 26; Ozja/Shutterstock Images, 27

Library of Congress Cataloging-in-Publication Data
Cataloging-in-publication information is on file with the Library of Congress.
978-1-63235-379-5 (hardcover)
978-1-63235-396-2 (paperback)
978-1-62143-520-4 (hosted ebook)

Printed in the United States of America
Mankato, MN
May, 2016

Access free, up-to-date content on this topic plus a full digital version of this book. Scan the QR code on page 31 or use your school's login at 12StoryLibrary.com.

Table of Contents

The Red List Is Growing

Thousands of animal species are threatened around the world. Understanding what puts these animals at risk allows humans to help the species survive. This knowledge also helps people identify other animals that may need help. All known threatened species are tracked on a list. Since 1964, the International Union for Conservation of Nature (IUCN) has kept its Red List.

Many countries and organizations keep their own lists. But the Red List attempts to include all threatened species in the world. It contains both animals and plants. Approximately 80,000 species are on the list. Some of these are in less danger than others. Some have already gone extinct. More than 20,000 species are currently threatened with extinction. Approximately 2,500 are critically endangered animals.

Those numbers continue to grow. Many animals face the same threats. Climate change and loss of living space are two of the biggest. One example of a species facing these threats is the polar bear. These bears rely on cold

Sea otters were nearly wiped out in the early 1900s due to the fur trade. They are still endangered.

Polar bears rely on sea ice to hunt seals.

environments. Polar bears hunt for food on sea ice, and it is melting. The IUCN expects the global polar bear population to drop by 30 percent over the next 35 to 40 years. But the polar bear is not alone. Many species large and small face similar threats.

The Red List is updated several times per year. It helps organizations around the world know what species need the most help.

834

Number of extinct animals on the Red List.

- The IUCN Red List has been kept since 1964.
- It helps track endangered species and spot others that could be at risk.
- Approximately 2,500 animals are critically endangered.
- Climate change and loss of habitat are two reasons the list is growing.

BACK FROM EXTINCTION

Some species seem to have risen from the dead. The coelacanth (SEE-luh-kanth) fish was thought to have disappeared along with dinosaurs 66 million years ago. Then one was caught near South Africa in 1938. They are hard to find, since they live down to 2,300 feet (700 m) deep in the ocean. The coelacanth is an endangered species. Approximately 1,000 exist in the world.

Endangered Species Act Has Been a Success

In 1914, the passenger pigeon went extinct. It used to be one of the most common birds in the United States. In 1944, the whooping crane was so endangered that only 21 of the birds were living. Pollution and pesticide use threatened many species in the 1950s and 1960s. Faced with these new threats, the US government decided to do something.

President Richard Nixon signed the Endangered Species Act (ESA) into law in 1973. The law was made to protect species and rebuild their populations. The ESA meets these goals in a few ways. The act identifies species that are endangered or threatened. It bans the hunting of these animals. Even accidentally hurting an animal on this list may be a crime. The ESA also makes sure the land these species live on is protected from damage by human activities.

The US government dedicates resources to protecting and recovering species. In the 40-plus-year history of the ESA, 98 percent of the species listed are still living. It takes a long time

AMERICA'S SYMBOL

One of the greatest success stories of the ESA is the bald eagle. The bald eagle is an official symbol of the United States. Fewer than 500 nesting pairs were alive in the 1960s. Strict hunting rules were put in place due to the ESA. Scientists developed ways to breed bald eagles. The eagles could then be released into the wild. The bird was removed from the list in 2007.

for a species to completely recover. Once a species has recovered, it is removed from the list. Compared with the number of species that have been listed, the number of those removed after recovery is small. However, many species still on the list are in stronger positions than they once were.

For example, in 1990, fewer than 50 green sea turtles were estimated to live along Florida's coastline, one of their main habitats. Thanks to the ESA, during the most recent count, in 2013, more than 10,000 nests were found on Florida beaches. Fewer than 500 El Segundo blue butterflies were known to exist in 1984. But their population has

since increased more than 20,000 percent. There are now more than 123,000 of these butterflies.

29
Number of species removed from the ESA list.

- Extinctions and threats encouraged government action in the first half of the 1900s.
- The Endangered Species Act became law in 1973.
- It protects species and encourages their regrowth.
- Approximately 98 percent of species protected by the ESA have not gone extinct.

Green sea turtles need space on beaches to nest.

National Wildlife Refuges Protect Endangered Species

Wildlife refuges are areas designated to protect certain plants and animals. Activities such as hunting and fishing may be limited or banned in these areas. The National Wildlife Refuge System goes back more than 100 years. President Theodore Roosevelt dedicated the first refuge in Florida in 1903. There are now more than 560 refuges. Every US state has at least one. People in most major American cities live within an hour's drive of a wildlife refuge.

These refuges are important for preserving species' habitats. Loss of habitat is a big reason species go extinct. According to the ESA, wildlife refuges protect nearly 400 threatened or endangered plant and animal species. Additionally, many non-endangered birds stop in refuges during their migrations.

Animal and plant species need refuges now more than ever. The human population is rising. Pollution is increasing. Cities are growing.

The first US wildlife refuge, Pelican Island, was started to help save the brown pelican.

AREA BEYOND THIS SIGN CLOSED
All public a tie prohibited

Chincoteague National Wildlife Refuge protects one of the few wild horse populations in the United States.

These factors allow less living space for animals.

Refuges also help humans. Refuges are large areas of land with little human presence. That helps humans living nearby live in less polluted environments with clean water.

The United States is not alone in these efforts. Almost every country on Earth has protected areas. These areas cover approximately 15 percent of Earth's surface, both land and sea. From 1990 to 2014, the size of protected areas went up significantly. The total area went from approximately 5 million square miles (13 million sq. km) to 12.4 million square miles (32 million sq. km). But just having these areas is not enough. Much work goes into maintaining them and making sure they protect wildlife.

234,375
Total area, in square miles (607,028 sq. km), of the US National Wildlife Refuge System.

- President Theodore Roosevelt dedicated the first national wildlife refuge in 1903.
- Approximately 400 endangered or threatened species live on US wildlife refuges.
- With expanding human populations, refuges preserve animal habitats.
- Other countries also have protected wildlife areas.

Reducing Pollution Saves Habitats

All animals and plants need space in order to live. One of the biggest reasons species become endangered is because they start to run out of living space. They run out of places to find food and make shelter. A major cause of habitat loss is pollution. Humans are the cause of pollution. It makes areas unlivable and puts all life in those areas at risk.

Increased manufacturing can mean more harmful materials enter the environment. This is especially bad for species living in water. Water can become so polluted that fish and other species can no longer live in it. In turn, species that eat plants and animals living in polluted water also suffer.

Some types of pollution also increase climate change. These pollutants trap heat in the atmosphere. Plants and animals have adapted to live at certain temperatures. Warmer temperatures put some species in danger. One of these is the American pika. Pikas are relatives of rabbits. The American pika lives in cold conditions at high elevations. These small animals can die if temperatures reach 78 degrees Fahrenheit (26°C). They have had to flee habitats in search of cooler conditions.

The San Joaquin kit fox is another species affected by human activity.

Litter is one form of pollution that harms the environment.

It lives throughout the central valley of California. The species used to be very common. Now there are fewer than 7,000 left. Humans have used pesticides in California to kill mice and other rodents. Kit foxes eat these rodents. Fewer rodents mean less food for kit foxes. Pesticides can also build up in kit foxes' bodies over time and kill them. By reducing human impact on the environment, animals will have more resources to thrive.

40,000
Percentage the world's chemical production increased from 1930 to 2000.

- Loss of habitat is a main reason animals go extinct.
- Pollution is a major cause of habitat loss.
- Humans create a lot of pollution, especially from manufacturing.
- Manufacturing also increases climate change, which can make animals abandon habitats.

Human development has shrunk the San Joaquin kit fox's habitat.

Endangered Species Are Threatened by Poaching

The illegal killing of plants and animals is called poaching. Many species become endangered because of poaching. Animals are often killed for their fur. Or they might be killed for other parts, such as teeth and claws, that can be made into products. Poaching does not affect only the animal killed. It can impact the entire environment the animal lives in.

Elephant tusks are made of a material called ivory. Ivory can be used to make jewelry and other items. Poachers in Asia and Africa kill a lot of elephants to take their tusks. Thousands of elephants are killed each year for their tusks. Rhinoceros horns are also in demand. People in some countries believe the horns can be used as medicine. Partly because of this,

the western black rhino went extinct in 2011.

Poaching is a serious problem. Organizations around the world are fighting it. Many countries have banned the sale of ivory. Others have stepped up efforts to inform people about not buying products that come from endangered animals. Animals can also be relocated into protected areas. But poachers

THE IVORY TRADE

Ivory was once used for all sorts of products. It was used to make piano keys until the 1970s. It is now illegal to sell ivory. In 2013, the US Fish and Wildlife Service held an event to crush more than six tons of ivory so it could not possibly be sold. The agency held another ivory crush in 2015.

sometimes still manage to get to them.

There are high-tech solutions, too. Poachers kill more than 1,000 rhinos in South Africa each year. Some rhinos have been fitted with a tiny camera inside their horns. It has sensors that can detect a change in heart rate. If the rhino is under stress from nearby poachers, a team can arrive in minutes to help. That can be quick enough to catch the fleeing poachers.

6

Average number of hours between rhino poachings in South Africa.

- Poaching is the illegal killing of a plant or animal.
- Poachers kill animals usually because they have high value.
- Countries have banned the sale of certain items that come from endangered animals and tell people not to buy them.
- Tiny cameras inside rhino horns can alert authorities to catch poachers in the act.

Elephants use their tusks for protection, digging, and gathering food.

6

Zoos Raise Awareness about Endangered Species

Zoos are wonderful places to see endangered species. In many cases, it might be the only chance people get to see these animals. Zoos help educate people about why species are in trouble. They show guests ways they can help. But zoos also do some of this help themselves.

Many members of the Association of Zoos and Aquariums (AZA) participate in its Species Survival Plan (SSP) program. This program tries to rebuild populations through breeding in captivity. But the main goal is not just to breed more animals. It is to have enough to send them back into the wild.

One example of a species brought back by the SSP is the California condor. There were only 23 known California condors in the wild in 1982. Thanks in part to

AZA members, nearly 200 condors now live in the wild. And many more live in AZA zoos. SSP efforts also helped the red wolf. Only 14 red wolves were known to live in the wild in the late 1970s. They were all captured in 1980 to try to restore the population. Point Defiance Zoo in Washington started a long-term program in 1984. Today, more than 30 facilities breed red wolves. More than 100 red wolves are now in the wild.

590
Number of species currently involved in the SSP.

- Many endangered species live in zoos.
- Zoos help people see which animals need help.
- Many zoos participate in programs to send endangered species back into the wild.
- The California condor is one species that was reintroduced into the wild due to zoo efforts.

THINK ABOUT IT

There are benefits to having endangered species in zoos. But some people believe the animals should remain free in the wild. What do you think is best for endangered species? Is it fair to them to keep them confined in zoos?

Invasive Species Play a Role

Invasive species are closely connected to endangered species. A plant or animal is invasive if it causes harm to an environment it is not originally from. Approximately 42 percent of threatened or endangered species are at risk due to invasive species. These species can damage their new habitats in a number of ways.

Invasive species usually spread due to human activity. They catch a ride on ships or in planes. They enter new environments and can throw off the balance of the ecosystem. They might not have any predators in the new environment. They might breed out of control and force other species out. Or they might eat too much of something and not leave enough for other species.

The Asian carp used to live only in Asia. It was introduced into the United States in the 1970s. It multiplies quickly and takes food

Burmese pythons are invasive species in Florida. They prey on mammals such as rabbits, deer, and bobcats.

from native fish. Plants can also be invasive. The water hyacinth is a plant that was bred for decoration. But in the wild, it grows very thick. It blocks sunlight from reaching other plants and wildlife.

The US Fish and Wildlife Service (FWS) has many methods to control invasive species. FWS workers might spray chemicals that kill only invasive plants. Or for invasive animals, they might release predators of that species.

Regular people can help, too. People should keep an eye out for invasive species, especially plants. If you spot one, telling your local FWS can help it stop the species from spreading.

$138 billion

Estimated cost per year of invasive species on the US economy.

- Invasive species are any species not native to where they are living.
- Invasive species are usually spread by human activity.
- They take up food and resources from other species.
- People should keep an eye out for invasive species to help stop their spread.

Asian carp often jump out of the water when approached by boats.

The COTSbot
Saves Coral Reefs

Coral reefs might look like a bunch of colorful rocks. But the reefs are actually made up of many small living organisms. Coral reefs face a number of threats. Human activity and climate change are major ones. But one small thing can do a lot of damage: a starfish.

The crown-of-thorns starfish (COTS) is native to coral reefs. But its numbers are increasing, partly due to overfishing of its natural predators. It feeds on coral. The Great Barrier Reef off the coast of Australia is the world's largest reef. The COTS is one of its biggest threats. So scientists at Queensland University of Technology in Australia started working on a solution.

The COTSbot is a robot that targets the COTS. The robot moves back and forth along the reef looking for them. It has cameras that know what to look for. It correctly identifies the starfish 99.4 percent of the time. When it finds one, it injects the COTS with poison. Just two teaspoons (10 mL) kill the starfish

Crown-of-thorns starfish have sharp spikes.

Using COTSbot is much easier than having divers remove the starfish.

21

Percentage of coral cover on the Great Barrier Reef lost due to the COTS from 1985 to 2012.

- Coral reefs are made up of living creatures.
- The crown-of-thorns starfish eats coral.
- Scientists in Australia designed the COTSbot to kill starfish that feed on coral in the Great Barrier Reef.
- The COTSbot poisons starfish, which die within 24 hours.

within 24 hours. Killing starfish helps control the population. A single starfish can make a million new starfish all by itself. The COTSbot can kill up to 200 starfish in one mission.

The Great Barrier Reef lost half of its coral between 1985 and 2012. The COTSbot is helping coral make a comeback in some areas of the reef.

Robots Spy on the Sage Grouse

The sage grouse used to be a very common bird in the western United States. In the 1800s, settlers said the birds were so numerous they made the sky dark when they flew. But by the 1950s, their population had declined in a big way.

As its name suggests, the sage grouse lives in sagebrush. Sagebrush used to cover 155 million acres (63 million ha) in the United States. Since then, sagebrush has declined 44 percent. The sage grouse population has decreased 90 percent in some areas since the 1970s. Fewer than 250,000 birds are alive today.

To figure out how to breed sage grouses, scientists needed to understand the species better. They needed to see the birds up close. Since 2008, robots have gone where

Male sage grouses fan their tails and puff up their chests to attract females.

The sage grouse robot moves by rolling along a small track.

humans could not. Scientists at the University of California, Davis, designed a robot disguised to look like a sage grouse. It carries a camera and a microphone.

The robot allows scientists to study the birds' behavior up close. Researchers have learned about how the birds communicate. They found that noise from human activities, such as oil drilling, can disrupt the grouses' communication. Birds in noisy areas are less likely to reproduce.

Because of the robot, scientists are now able to help make the best possible environment for the sage grouse. This information might also be useful for other similar birds.

16
Sound intensity, in decibels, of the ideal sagebrush environment for grouses—quieter than a whisper.

- The sage grouse used to be one of North America's most common birds.
- These birds used to number in the millions, but fewer than 250,000 are still alive.
- Scientists designed a robot to observe the grouse up close.
- They learned about how grouses communicate and how noise can disrupt their lives.

10

To Save a Crane, Dress Like One

The dodo and the passenger pigeon are two famous birds that have gone extinct. The whooping crane almost joined them in the 1940s. Approximately 24 individuals were left. Thanks to the work of several groups, there are now more than 450 in the wild. One of these groups is the International Crane Foundation (ICF).

The ICF hopes to help build a flock of approximately 120 cranes. The goal is to get them to migrate between Florida and Wisconsin. This project will take years to achieve. To grow the population, ICF members must raise the birds themselves. Young cranes depend on their mothers. But there aren't enough adult cranes to raise the population quickly. So the scientists must dress like female cranes.

It starts with an all-white suit. Then there's a hand puppet that looks like a crane beak. Scientists feed the

The whooping crane is the tallest bird in North America.

young cranes using this beak, just as their mothers would. The young cranes also follow the lead of the puppet. They know what to do based on their "mother's" behavior. This is how they learn to fly.

The scientists can't teach the young birds every lesson their parents would. But the ICF can set them up to survive in the wild. When the crane costumes fail, scientists have other ideas. They use adult

Scientists use puppets to mimic crane behavior.

8

Average width, in feet (2.4 m), of the wingspan of an adult whooping crane.

- Approximately 24 whooping cranes remained in the 1940s.
- More than 450 whooping cranes are alive today.
- Cranes learn from their mothers how to fly and eat.
- To simulate this relationship, scientists dress like cranes to raise the young birds into adults.

cranes in captivity to play the role of parents. Even though they are not the cranes' actual mothers, adult cranes can train the baby birds better than humans.

The success of the ICF project depends on how well the cranes are raised. Only time will tell if it is effective. But the migrating population is increasing each year.

"Frozen Zoo" Could Help Rebuild Species

The University of Georgia contains a very special kind of zoo. The animals in this zoo aren't alive. They aren't even grown yet. The "frozen zoo" contains the cells of several endangered species.

Cells are the basic units of life. They can last a long time when frozen. Future technology may allow scientists to grow species using these frozen cells. Currently, scientists rely on breeding endangered species to produce more. But this is difficult, and it produces only a few new animals. Creating animals from cells could produce thousands of individuals. It could totally rebuild a population.

People at the frozen zoo hope to get cell samples from many endangered species. Right now, the facility is focusing on big cats.

Its first two came from a Sumatran tiger and a clouded leopard. The Sumatran tiger is very endangered. Approximately 400 remain.

Two challenges remain for the project's scientists. They must continue to work on their technology. And they need funding. Their goal

THE DWINDLING WHITE RHINO

One of the most recent animals to have its cells frozen was the northern white rhino. After one died in December 2015 at a San Diego–area zoo, scientists rushed to gather its cells. That's because after the rhino's death, only five were left in the world. None of these are able to reproduce. The cells collected may be the only hope for the northern white rhino's future survival.

The clouded leopard is named for its cloud-like spots.

78
Percentage of Sumatran tiger deaths from poaching— approximately 40 deaths per year.

- Future technology may allow scientists to rebuild species from their cells.
- A facility in Georgia is currently storing the cells of endangered species.
- The Sumatran tiger and the clouded leopard were the first two species to have their frozen cells kept there.
- Unlike traditional breeding, this method could produce thousands of animals.

is to educate people on the threat facing animals like the Sumatran tiger. They hope to get donations from people to help save these animals. If all goes as planned, the tiger may never go extinct.

THINK ABOUT IT

Some people argue that creating animals from cells would be unnatural and wrong. But it could mean the survival of a species. What do you think? Do you think it's worth it?

De-extinction May One Day Be Possible

The woolly mammoth was a giant, furry elephant. It went extinct more than 4,000 years ago. It roamed the coldest parts of Earth. When some of these animals died, they ended up frozen in the ground. That meant their bodies were well preserved. Scientists now believe they could make new mammoths.

Unlike the Sumatran tiger, the mammoth is no longer around for scientists to sample. Scientists have had to re-create the mammoth's DNA. DNA is the unique code that determines all the features of living things. Scientists may be able to use this code with modern elephants to create a new mammoth.

The technology does not exist today. But some scientists believe it could happen within a few years. In 2015, researchers at Harvard University implanted mammoth DNA into the cells of an Asian elephant. Since the animals are similar, it is the first step in seeing if it is possible to grow a mammoth. The experiment was successful. Mammoth genes were active in living cells for the first time in 4,000 years.

A living, breathing mammoth is still a long way off. But in the future, a species long gone from Earth could actually roam the planet once again.

It's not just the woolly mammoth. With the same theory, scientists could resurrect any extinct species if they had its DNA. They could then use a living relative—such as an

DNA carries living things' genetic information.

24,000

Estimated weight, in pounds (11,000 kg), of the heaviest woolly mammoths.

- The woolly mammoth was an ancestor of the elephant that went extinct more than 4,000 years ago.
- Many mammoths froze in the ground after death and were well preserved.
- Scientists were able to resurrect their genetic code.
- This code, called DNA, could one day help create new mammoths.

elephant for a mammoth—to give birth. But unlike in the movies, dinosaurs probably aren't coming back. There isn't enough DNA from 66 million years ago. But more recent extinct species, such as the passenger pigeon, could one day return to Earth.

The reason for the woolly mammoth's extinction is unknown.

27

Fact Sheet

- The number of species that go extinct each year is not known for sure. It depends on how many species there are on Earth. That number also isn't known for sure. Estimates of the total number of species range from 2 million to more than 100 million. The extinction rate is between 0.01 and 0.10 percent per year. That means anywhere from 200 to 100,000 species may be going extinct each year.

- Among all animal groups, snails and slugs have gone extinct more than any other. A total of 281 species from the group are known to have gone extinct.

- The Loneliest palm tree is the most endangered plant in the world. Only one exists in the world, on the island country of Mauritius. Attempts to reproduce the plant have so far not been successful.

- Sharks are one of the world's most threatened types of animals. One-third of all sharks are at risk of extinction. Between 26 and 73 million sharks are killed each year for their fins. Shark fins are believed to be medicinal in some parts of the world.

- The Javan rhinoceros is one of the most endangered individual animals. It went extinct in Vietnam in 2010, leaving only one group left in the world. Fewer than 50 Javan rhinos exist. They live on the island of Java in Indonesia.

Glossary

captivity
The state of being held or kept in a place.

climate
Long-term weather conditions on Earth.

extinct
When no individuals from a species exist on Earth.

funding
Money kept for a special purpose.

habitat
The area in which a species of plant or animal lives.

migration
When a group of animals travels across a distance together.

native
A species that lives or grows naturally in a certain place.

pollution
Harmful material introduced into the environment.

predator
An animal that hunts other animals for food.

refuge
A safe place protected from harmful effects.

species
A specific type of animal or plant.

wildlife
All plants and animals that live in nature.

For More Information

Books

Boothroyd, Jennifer. *Endangered and Extinct Mammals*. Minneapolis, MN: Lerner, 2014.

Furstinger, Nancy. *12 Mammals Back from the Brink*. North Mankato, MN: Peterson, 2015.

Gagne, Tammy. *The Most Endangered Animals in the World*. Mankato, MN: Capstone, 2015.

Kalman, Bobbie. *Why and Where Are Animals Endangered?* New York: Crabtree, 2015.

Visit 12StoryLibrary.com

Scan the code or use your school's login at **12StoryLibrary.com** for recent updates about this topic and a full digital version of this book. Enjoy free access to:

- Digital ebook
- Breaking news updates
- Live content feeds
- Videos, interactive maps, and graphics
- Additional web resources

Note to educators: Visit 12StoryLibrary.com/register to sign up for free premium website access. Enjoy live content plus a full digital version of every 12-Story Library book you own for every student at your school.

Index

American pika, 10
Asian carp, 16
Association of Zoos and
    Aquariums (AZA), 14

bald eagle, 6

California condor, 14
climate change, 4, 10,
    18
clouded leopard, 24
coelacanth, 5
coral reef, 18–19
crown-of-thorns starfish
    (COTS), 18–19

DNA, 26–27
dodo, 22

elephant, 12, 26–27
El Segundo blue
    butterfly, 7
Endangered Species Act
    (ESA), 6–8

Fish and Wildlife Service,
    US (FWS), 12, 17

giant panda, 14
green sea turtle, 7

International Crane
    Foundation (ICF),
    22–23
invasive species, 16–17
IUCN Red List, 4–5

National Wildlife Refuge
    System, 8–9
Nixon, Richard, 6

passenger pigeon, 6, 22,
    27
pesticide, 6, 11
poaching, 12–13
polar bear, 4–5
pollution, 6, 8–10

red wolf, 14
rhinoceros, 12–13, 24
Roosevelt, Theodore, 8

sage grouse, 20–21
San Joaquin kit fox,
    10–11
Species Survival Plan
    (SSP), 14
Sumatran tiger, 24–26

whooping crane, 6,
    22–23
woolly mammoth, 26–27

About the Author

Todd Kortemeier is a writer from
Minneapolis, Minnesota. He is
a graduate of the University of
Minnesota's School of Journalism
& Mass Communication. He has
authored many books for young
people.

32

READ MORE FROM 12-STORY LIBRARY

Every 12-Story Library book
is available in many formats.
For more information, visit
12StoryLibrary.com.